Christmas Carols

with the Christmas Story
as told by St. Luke and St. Matthew
Compiled and arranged by

Frank Edwin Peat

Illustrated by

Fern Bisel Peat

Manuscript scores by
Wenzel Kubelka

The Saalfield Publishing Company
Akron, Ohio   New York

To

Muzzy and Puz

my mother and father, who
for so many years have told
the story of the Christ Child
to the people of the
Middle Kingdom

Foreword

A STARLIT NIGHT among the hills near Bethlehem. A glorious song—and the history of the world was changed.

Since that night when angels sang, Christians have celebrated the birth of Jesus Christ in songs of praise and worship, and today, all over the world, Christmas carols in every tongue fill the air as all Christendom unites in again proclaiming the coming of the Christ Child.

In the early days carols were sung by "waits," or bands of men and boys who went about the streets for several nights before Christmas, singing in the open air. Some of the carols in use today are examples of our oldest forms of musical expression, and our earliest hymns were, perhaps, those which repeated the words which the angels sang to the shepherds near Bethlehem,

Glory to God in the highest,
And on earth peace, good will toward men.

Many of the ancient carols were composed to commemorate the festivities or to retell some of the legendary stories and customs which have grown up around the celebrating of the Christmas season. Some of these carols were dance forms, from which the word "carol" is derived. Some were drinking and feasting songs, and others simple folk songs which only suggested the religious or treated a religious theme in a familiar and festive manner.

Christmas hymns are essentially devotional in character, and we find among them some of our most inspired expressions of Christian music. These hymns were written around the incidents of the coming of our Lord as recorded in the Gospels by St. Luke and St. Matthew. In the following pages this Christmas Story appears with the great hymns of Christmas so that we may follow the events in both story and song.

From the wealth of traditional music which has sprung from the hearts of men through the centuries, we have brought together a selection of the best known and most familiar carols. It is our hope that this collection will encourage the picturesque and delightful custom of singing together at Christmas time.

Frank E. Peat

The Christmas Story

PROPHECY

COMFORT ye, comfort ye my people, saith your God.

Speak ye comfortably to Jerusalem, and cry unto her that her warfare is accomplished, that her iniquity is pardoned.

The voice of him that crieth in the wilderness, Prepare ye the way of the Lord, make straight in the desert a highway for our God.

O Zion, that bringest good tidings, get thee up into the high mountain; O Jerusalem, that bringest good tidings, lift up thy voice with strength; lift it up, be not afraid; say unto the cities of Judah, Behold, your God.

Therefore the Lord himself shall give you a sign; Behold, a virgin shall conceive, and bear a son, and shall call his name Immanuel.

And there shall come forth a rod out of the stem of Jesse, and a Branch shall grow out of his roots:

And the Spirit of the Lord shall rest upon Him, the spirit of wisdom and understanding, the spirit of counsel and might, the spirit of knowledge and of the fear of the Lord.

With righteousness shall he judge the poor, and reprove with equity for the meek of the earth.

For unto us a child is born, unto us a son is given: and the government shall be upon his shoulder: and his name shall be called Wonderful, Counsellor, The mighty God, The everlasting Father, The Prince of Peace. —*Isaiah.*

Adeste Fideles

Anonymous. Latin, 18th century   Source unknown, 18th century melody

1. O come, all ye faith-ful, joy-ful and tri-umphant, O come ye, O
2. Sing, choirs of an-gels, sing in ex-ul-ta-tion, O sing, all ye
3. Yea, Lord, we greet Thee, born this happy morning, Je-sus, to

come ye to Beth-le-hem! Come and be-hold Him, born the King of an-gels!
cit-i-zens of heav'n a-bove! Glo-ry to God, all glo-ry in the high-est!
Thee be all glo-ry giv'n; Word of the Fa-ther, now in flesh ap-pear-ing!

Refrain

O come, let us a-dore Him, O come, let us a-dore Him, O come, let us a-

dore Him, Christ, the Lord! A——men.

FULFILMENT

AND it came to pass in those days, that there went out a decree from Caesar Augustus, that all the world should be taxed.

And all went to be taxed, every one into his own city.

And Joseph also went up from Galilee, out of the city of Nazareth, into Judea, unto the city of David, which is called Bethlehem; (because he was of the house and lineage of David;)

To be taxed with Mary his espoused wife, being great with child.

Once In Royal David's City

Mrs. C. F. Alexander.   H. J. Gauntlett.

And so it was, that, while they were there, the days were accomplished that she should be delivered.

And she brought forth her firstborn son, and wrapped him in swaddling clothes, and laid him in a manger, because there was no room for them in the inn.

Silent Night

Joseph Mohr.

Franz Grüber.

1. Si - lent night, ho - ly night, All is calm, all is bright;
2. Si - lent night, ho - ly night, Dark-ness flies, all is light;
3. Si - lent night, ho - ly night, Won-drous Star, lend thy light;

Round yon Vir - gin Moth-er and Child! Ho - ly In-fant, so ten-der and mild,
Shep-herds hear the an —gels sing, "Al - le-lu - ia! hail the King!
With the an-gels let us sing, Al - le lu - ia to our King;

Sleep in heaven-ly peace, Sleep in heaven-ly peace.
Christ the Saviour is born, Christ the Saviour is born."
Christ the Saviour is born, Christ the Saviour is born. A - men.

And there were in the same country shepherds abiding in the field,
keeping watch over their flock by night.

4 While Shepherds Watched Their Flocks

Nahum Tate

Arr. from George F. Händel.

1. While shep-herds watched their flocks by night, All
2. "Fear not!" said he—for might-y dread Had
3. "To you, in Da-vid's town this day, Is
4. "The heaven-ly Babe you there shall find To

seat-ed on the ground, The an-gel of the Lord came down,
seized their troubled mind "Glad ti-dings of great joy I bring,
born of Da-vid's line, The Sav-iour, who is Christ the Lord;
hu-man view dis-played, All mean-ly wrapped in swathing bands,

And glo-ry shone a-round, And glo-ry shone a-round.
To you and all man-kind, To you and all man-kind.
And this shall be the sign, And this shall be the sign:
And in a manger laid, And in a manger laid."

And, lo, the angel of the Lord came upon them, and the glory of the
Lord shone round about them: and they were sore afraid.

And the angel said unto them, Fear not: for, behold, I bring you good
tidings of great joy, which shall be to all people.

For unto you is born this day in the city of David a Saviour, which is Christ the Lord.

And this shall be a sign unto you; Ye shall find the babe wrapped in swaddling clothes, lying in a manger.

There's A Song In The Air!

Josiah G. Holland

Karl P. Harrington.

1. There's a song in the air! There's a star in the sky! There's a
2. There's a tu-mult of joy O'er the won-der-ful birth, For the
3. In the light of that star Lie the a-ges impearled; And that
4. We re-joice in the light, And we ech-o the song That comes

mother's deep prayer, And a baby's low cry! And the star rains its fire while the
Vir-gin's sweet boy Is the Lord of the earth. Ay! the star rains its fire while the
song from a-far Has swept o-ver the world. Every hearth is a-flame, and the
down thro' the night From the heaven-ly throng. Ay! we shout to the love-ly e-

beau-ti-ful sing, For the manger of Beth-le-hem cradles a King)!
beau-ti-ful sing, For the manger of Beth-le-hem cradles a King)!
beau-ti-ful sing In the homes of the nations that Je-sus is King)!
van-gel they bring, And we greet in His cra-dle our Saviour and King)!

Words used by permission of Charles Scribner's Sons.
Music used by permission of Karl P. Harrington.

And suddenly there was with the angel a multitude of the heavenly host praising God, and saying,
Glory to God in the highest, and on earth peace, good will toward men.

Fern Bisel Peat

It Came Upon The Midnight Clear

8

Edmund H. Sears

Richard S. Willis.

1. It came up-on the mid-night clear, That glo-rious song of old,
2. Still thro' the clo-ven skies they come, With peaceful wings un-furled,

From an-gels bend-ing near the earth, To touch their harps of gold:
And still their heavenly mu-sic floats O'er all the wea-ry world:

"Peace on the earth, good will to men, From heaven's all-gra-cious King."
A- bove its sad and low-ly plains They bend on hov-ering wing,

The world in sol-emn still-ness lay, To hear the an-gels sing.
And ev-er o'er its Ba-bel sounds The bless-ed an-gels sing.

And it came to pass, as the angels were gone away from them into heaven, the shepherds said one to another, Let us now go even unto Bethlehem, and see this thing which is come to pass, which the Lord hath made known unto us.

And they came with haste, and found Mary, and Joseph, and the babe lying in a manger.

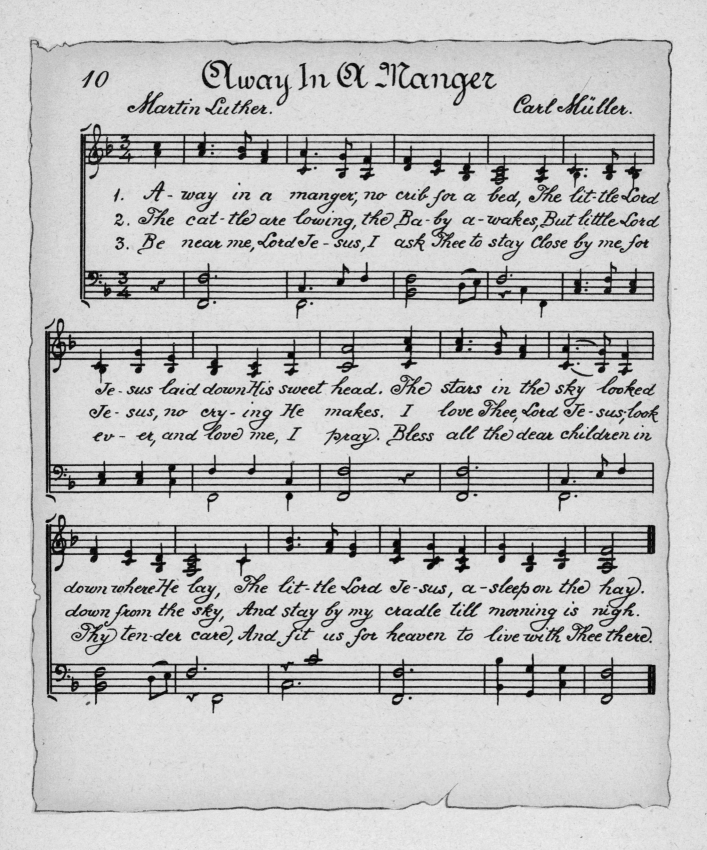

11 Gentle Mary Laid Her Child

Joseph S. Cook. 16th Century Carol.

1. Gen-tle Ma-ry laid her Child Low-ly in a man-ger;
2. An-gels sang a-bout His birth; Wise men sought and found Him;

There He lay, the un-de-filed, To the world a Stran-ger.
Heav-en's star shone brightly forth, Glo-ry all a-round Him.

Such a Babe in such a place, Can He be the Sav-iour?
Shepherds saw the wondrous sight, Heard the an-gels sing-ing;

Ask the saved of all the race Who have found His fa—vor.
All the plains were lit that night, All the hills were ring—ing.

Words used by permission of Alta Lind Cook
Music used by permission of Ernest Mac Millan.

And when they had seen it, they made known abroad the saying which was told them concerning this child.

And all they that heard it wondered at those things which were told them by the shepherds.

And the shepherds returned, glorifying and praising God for all the things that they had heard and seen, as it was told unto them.

—*St. Luke.*

NOW when Jesus was born in Bethlehem of Judea in the days of Herod the king, behold, there came wise men from the east to Jerusalem, Saying, Where is he that is born King of the Jews? for we have seen his star in the east, and are come to worship him.

The Kings Of The East

Katharine Lee Bates.   Clarence G. Hamilton

14

1. The Kings of the East are rid-ing To-night to Beth-le-hem;
2. To a strange sweet song of Zi-on The star-ry host troops forth:

The sun-set glows di-vid-ing, The Kings of the East are rid-ing,
The golden glaived O-ri-on To a strange sweet song of Zi-on,

A star their journey guiding, Gleaming with gold and gem.
The Archer and the Li-on, The watchers of the North:

The Kings of the East are riding Tonight to Beth-le-hem.
To a strange sweet song of Zi-on The star-ry host troops forth.

Words used by permission of Houghton Mifflin Company
Music used by permission of Clarence G. Hamilton

When Herod the king had heard these things, he was troubled, and all Jerusalem with him.

And when he had gathered all the chief priests and scribes of the people together, he demanded of them where Christ should be born.

And they said unto him, In Bethlehem of Judea: for thus it is written by the prophet,

And thou Bethlehem, art not the least among the princes of Judah: for out of thee shall come a Governor, that shall rule my people Israel.

And, lo, the star, which they saw in the east, went before them,
till it came and stood over where the young child was.

When they saw the star, they rejoiced with exceeding great
joy.

Fern Bisel Peat

And when they were come into the house, they saw the young child with Mary his mother, and fell down, and worshipped him: and when they had opened their treasures, they presented unto him gifts; gold, and frankincense, and myrrh.

—*St. Matthew.*

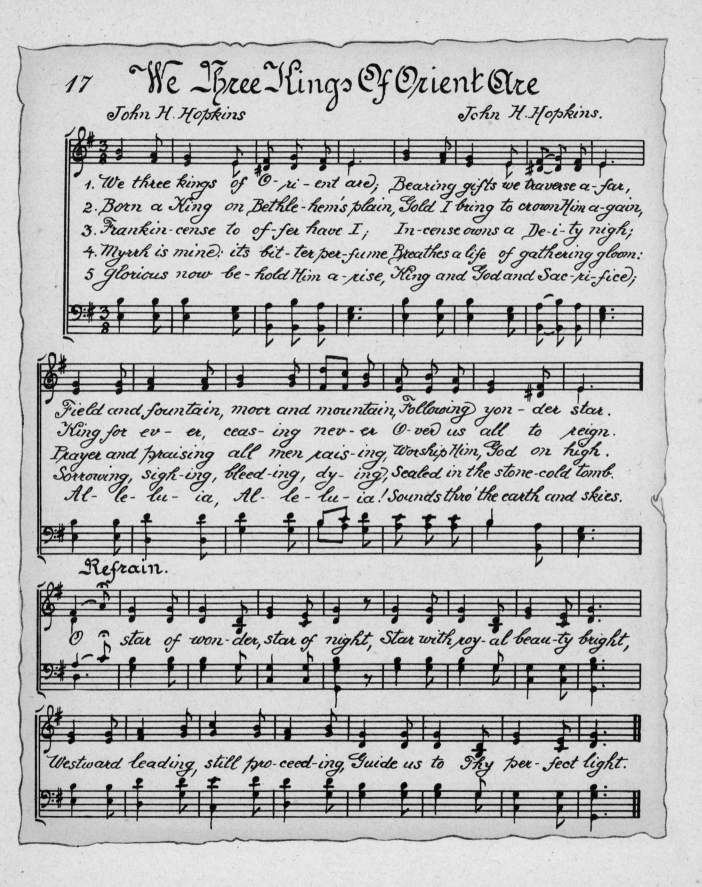

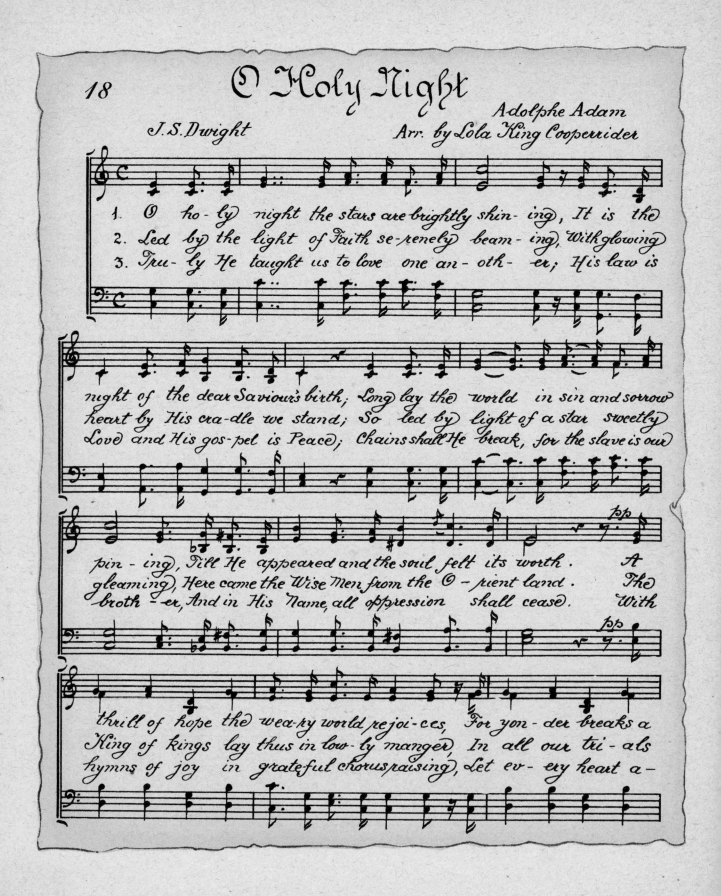

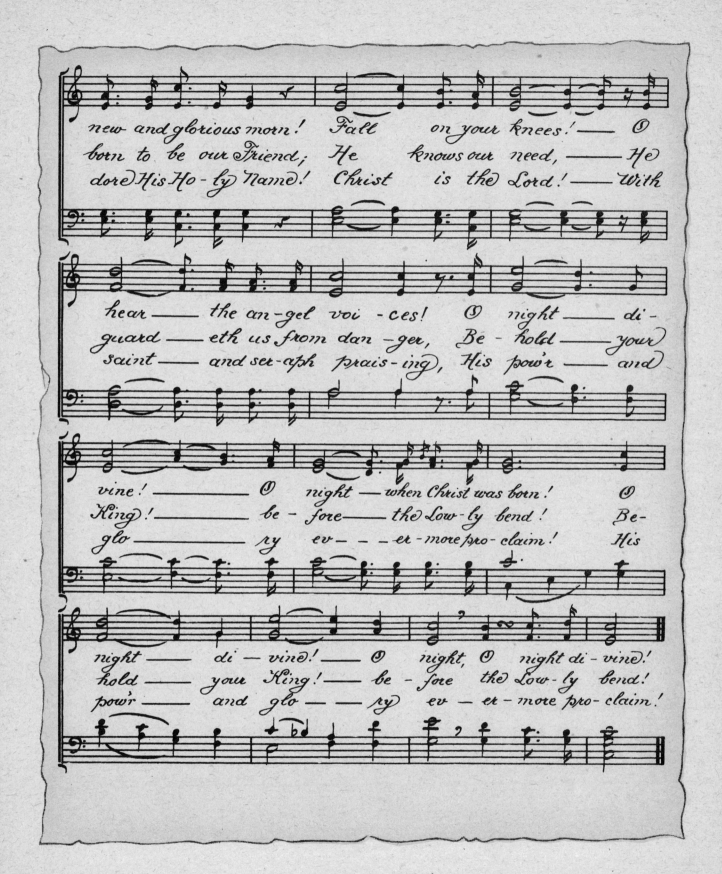

Traditional Carols

19 I Heard The Bells On Christmas Day

Henry Wadsworth Longfellow   Isaac H. Meredith

1. I heard the bells on Christmas Day Their old fa - mil - iar
2. I thought how as the day had come, The bel - fries of all
3. And in de - spair I bowed my head, - There is no peace on
4. Then pealed the bells more loud and deep, - God is not dead, and
5. Till ring - ing, sing - ing on its way The world re - volved from

car - ols play; And wild and sweet the word re - peat Of
Chris - ten - dom Had rolled a - long th'un - brok - en song Of
earth, I said, For hate is strong, and mocks the song Of
doth not sleep; The wrong shall fail, the right pre - vail With
night to day, A voice, a chime, a chant sublime Of.

peace on earth, good will to men.
peace on earth, good will to men.
peace on earth, good will to men.
peace on earth, good will to men.
peace on earth, good will to men.

Music used by permission of Tullar Meredith Company.

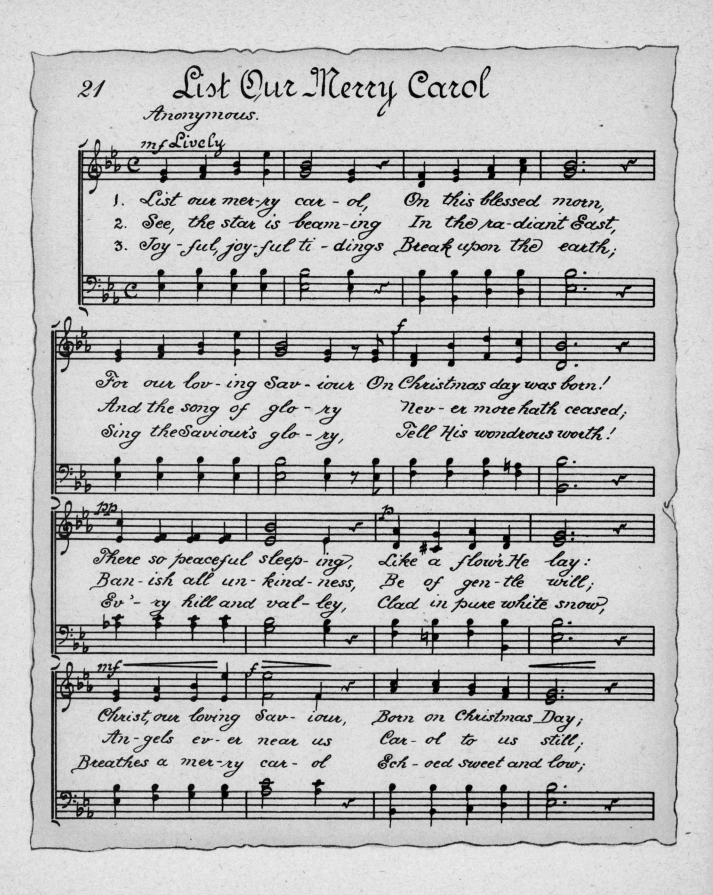

21 List Our Merry Carol

Anonymous.

mf Lively

1. List our mer-ry car-ol, On this blessed morn,
2. See, the star is beam-ing In the ra-diant East,
3. Joy-ful, joy-ful ti-dings Break upon the earth;

For our lov-ing Sav-iour On Christmas day was born!
And the song of glo-ry Nev-er more hath ceased;
Sing the Saviour's glo-ry, Tell His wondrous worth!

There so peaceful sleep-ing, Like a flow'r He lay:
Ban-ish all un-kind-ness, Be of gen-tle will;
Ev'-ry hill and val-ley, Clad in pure white snow,

Christ, our loving Sav-iour, Born on Christmas Day;
An-gels ev-er near us Car-ol to us still;
Breathes a mer-ry car-ol Ech-oed sweet and low;

List Our Merry Carol (Continued)

Christ, our lov-ing Sav-iour,   Born on Christmas Day.
An-gels ev-er near us   Car-ol to us still.
Breathes a mer-ry car-ol   Ech-oed sweet and low.

Chorus

Car-ol, car-ol gai-ly,   Car-ol on our way,

Christ, our loving Sav-iour,   Born on Christmas Day.

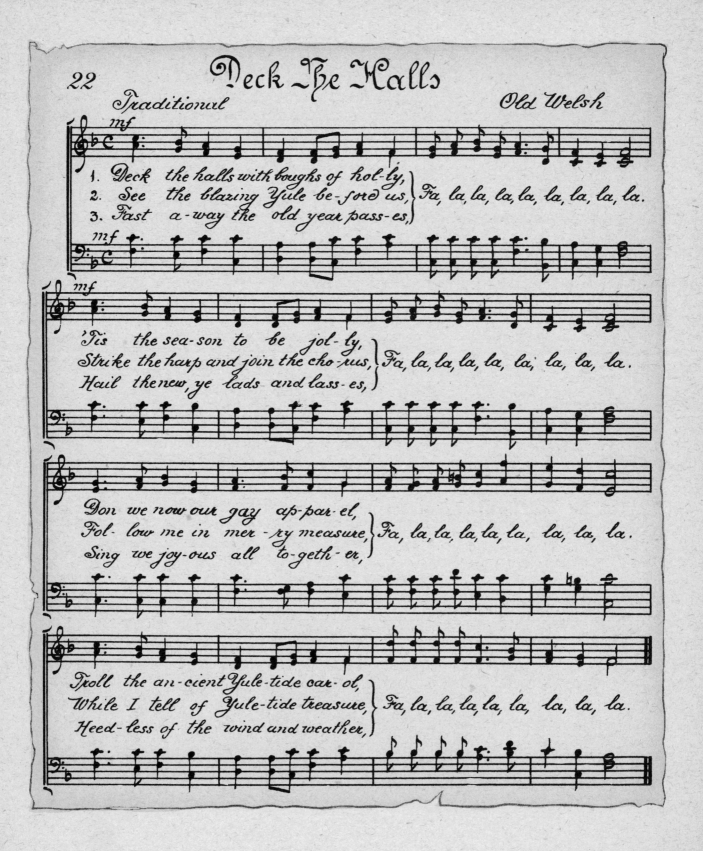

Deck The Halls

Traditional

Old Welsh

1. Deck the halls with boughs of hol-ly,
2. See the blazing Yule be-fore us,
3. Fast a-way the old year pass-es,
Fa, la, la, la, la, la, la, la, la.

'Tis the sea-son to be jol-ly,
Strike the harp and join the cho-rus,
Hail the new, ye lads and lass-es,
Fa, la, la, la, la, la, la, la, la.

Don we now our gay ap-par-el,
Fol-low me in mer-ry measure,
Sing we joy-ous all to-geth-er,
Fa, la, la, la, la, la, la, la, la.

Troll the an-cient Yule-tide car-ol,
While I tell of Yule-tide treasure,
Heed-less of the wind and weather,
Fa, la, la, la, la, la, la, la, la.

Christmas Is Here

Traditional.   English.

1. Sing we all mer-ri-ly,— Christmas is here,— Day that we
2. Sing we all joy-ful-ly,— sing of Christ's birth,— Sing what the

love best of days in our year; Bring forth the hol-ly, the
an-gels sang, "Peace up-on earth!" Par-ents and children in

box and the bay,— Deck out the cot-tage for glad Christmas day.
bright garments dress'd, Hasten to church to sing praise with the rest.

Chorus.

Christmas is here, Christmas is here, Sing we all merri-ly Christmas is here;

Christmas is here, Christmas is here, Sing we all merrily, Christ-mas is here.

O Tannenbaum

Traditional German

1. O Christmas Tree, O Christmas Tree, Thy leaves are green forever. O
2. O Christmas Tree, O Christmas Tree, Aflame with lights and splendor. O
3. O Christmas Tree, O Christmas Tree, Thy beauty doth remind us. O

Christmas Tree, O Christmas Tree, Thy leaves are green for-ev-er. They
Christmas Tree, O Christmas Tree, Aflame with lights and splendor. Thy
Christmas Tree, O Christmas Tree, Thy beauty doth re-mind us. Tho'

all are green in summer's prime, They all are green at Christmas time. O
boughs shine forth with candles' glow, And flash on eager eyes below. O
hearts are filled with joy and mirth, We hail today the Saviour's birth. O

Christmas Tree, O Christmas Tree, Thy leaves are green for-ev-er.
Christmas Tree, O Christmas Tree, Aflame with lights and splendor.
Christmas Tree, O Christmas Tree, Thy beauty doth re-mind us.

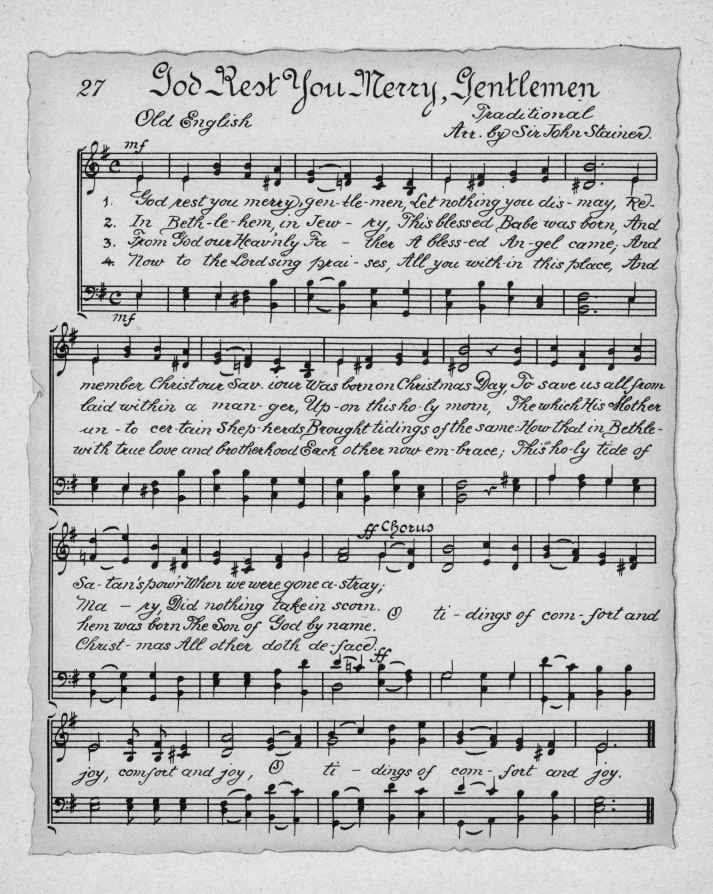

28 Caroll Of Bryngyng In The Bore's Heed

Old Oxford Carol.

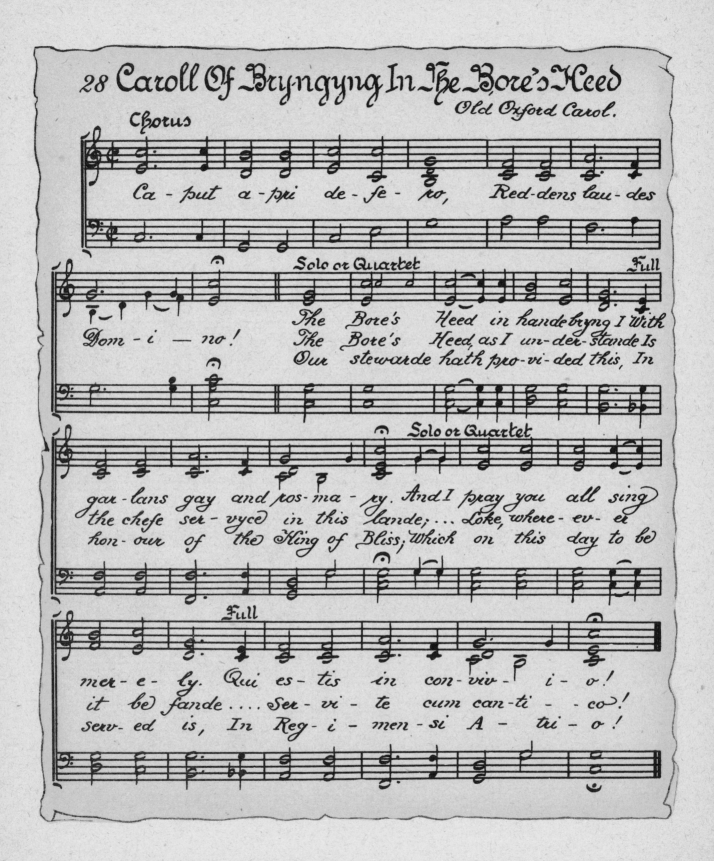

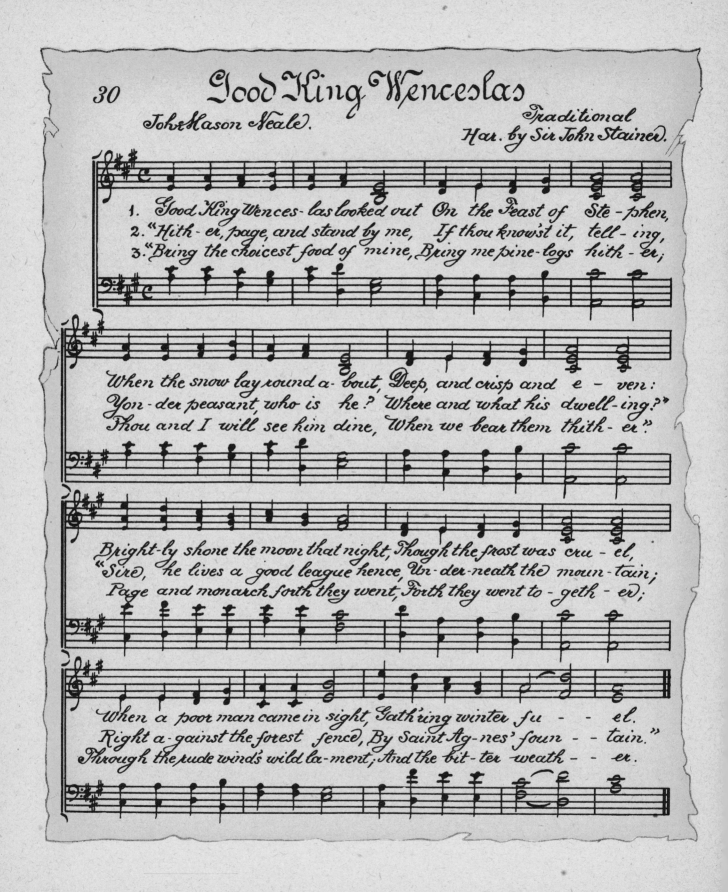

Listen, Lordlings, Unto Me (Continued)

Wea-ry were they, nigh to death; and for a lodging pray'd. Sing high, sing

Pur-er than the drops of dew and brighter than the morn. sing high,

At the al-tar Him to find who lay within the stall.

low, Sing high, sing low, sing to and fro, Go tell it out with

sing low,

speed, Cry out, and shout all round about That Christ is born in-deed.

I Saw Three Ships

Traditional

English
Arranged by Sir John Stainer

1. I saw three ships come sailing in, On Christmas Day, on Christmas Day; I
2. And what was in those ships all three, On Christmas Day, on Christmas Day? And
3. The Vir-gin Mary and Christ were there, On Christmas Day on Christmas Day; The

saw three ships come sailing in, On Christmas Day in the morn-ing.
what was in those ships all three, On Christmas Day in the morn-ing?
Vir-gin Mary and Christ were there, On Christmas Day in the morn-ing.

4. Pray, whither sailed those ships all three,
   On Christmas Day, on Christmas Day?
   Pray, whither sailed those ships all three,
   On Christmas Day in the morning?

5. O they sailed into Bethlehem,
   On Christmas Day, on Christmas Day;
   O they sailed into Bethlehem,
   On Christmas Day in the morning.

6. And all the bells on earth shall ring,
   On Christmas Day, on Christmas Day;
   And all the bells on earth shall ring,
   On Christmas Day in the morning.

7. Then let us all rejoice amain,
   On Christmas Day, on Christmas Day;
   Then let us all rejoice amain,
   On Christmas Day in the morning.

The Golden Carol

Old English

34

1. We saw a light shine out a-far, On Christmas in the morning, And

2. Oh! ev-er thought be of His Name, On Christmas in the morning, Who

straight we knew it was Christ's star, Bright beaming in the morning. Then

bore) for us both grief and shame, Af-flic-tions sharpest scorning. And

did we fall on bend-ed knee, On Christmas in the morning, And

may we die (when death shall come,) On Christmas in the morning, And

praised the Lord, who'd let us see His glo-ry at its dawning.

see in heav'n, our glorious home, That Star of Christmas morning.

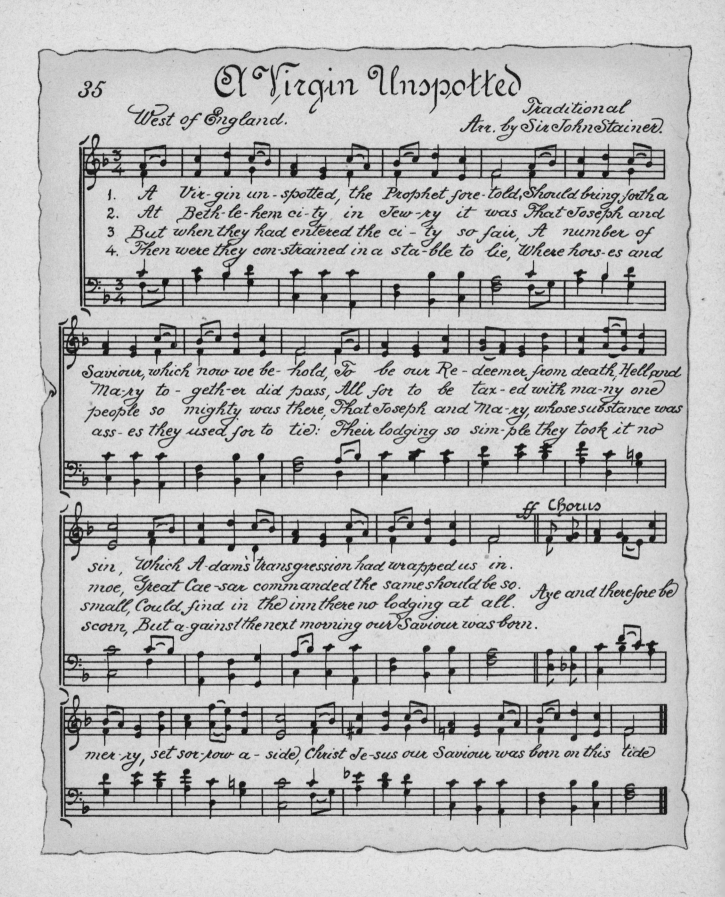

5. The King of all kings to this world being brought,
   Small store of fine linen to wrap Him was sought;
   But when she had swaddled her young Son so sweet,
   Within an ox manger she laid Him to sleep.
             Aye and therefore, etc.

6. Then God sent an angel from Heaven so high,
   To certain poor shepherds in fields where they lie,
   And bade them no longer in sorrow to stay,
   Because that our Saviour was born on this day.
             Aye and therefore, etc.

7. To teach us humility all this was done,
   And learn we from thence haughty pride for to shun:
   A manger His cradle who came from above,
   The great God of mercy, of peace, and of love.
             Aye and therefore, etc.

36   Carol Of The Birds

Bas-Quercey   Bas-Quercey

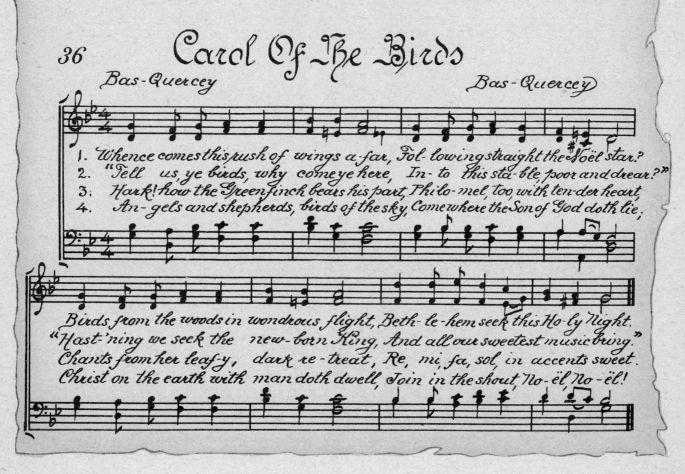

1. Whence comes this rush of wings afar, Following straight the Noël star?
2. "Tell us, ye birds, why come ye here, Into this stable poor and drear?"
3. Hark! how the Greenfinch bears his part, Philomel, too, with tender heart,
4. Angels and shepherds, birds of the sky, Come where the Son of God doth lie;

Birds from the woods in wondrous flight, Bethlehem seek this Holy Night.
"Hast'ning we seek the new-born King, And all our sweetest music bring."
Chants from her leafy, dark retreat, Re, mi, fa, sol, in accents sweet.
Christ on the earth with man doth dwell, Join in the shout, No-ël, No-ël!

The Seven Joys of Mary

English
Arranged by Sir John Stainer

1. The first good joy that Mary had, It was the joy of one; — To see the bless-ed Je-sus Christ, When He was first her Son. — When He was first her Son, Good Lord;

2. The next good joy that Mary had, It was the joy of two; — To see her own Son Je-sus Christ Mak-ing the lame to go. — Mak-ing the lame to go, Good Lord; And happy may we be; —— Praise

3. The next good joy that Mary had, It was the joy of three; — To see her own Son Je-sus Christ Mak-ing the blind to see. — Mak-ing the blind to see, Good Lord;

Refrain

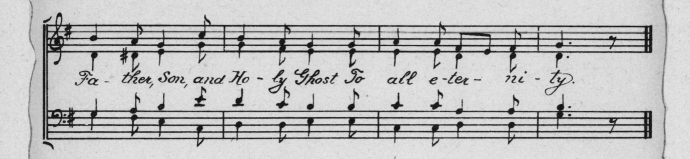

Fa - ther, Son, and Ho - ly Ghost To all e - ter - ni - ty.

4. The next good joy that Mary had,
   It was the joy of four;
   To see her own Son Jesus Christ
   Reading the Bible o'er.
   Reading the Bible o'er, Good Lord;
       And happy, etc.

6. The next good joy that Mary had,
   It was the joy of six;
   To see her own Son Jesus Christ
   Upon the Crucifix.
   Upon the Crucifix, Good Lord;
       And happy, etc.

5. The next good joy that Mary had,
   It was the joy of five;
   To see her own Son Jesus Christ
   Raising the dead to life.
   Raising the dead to life, Good Lord;
       And happy, etc.

7. The next good joy that Mary had,
   It was the joy of seven;
   To see her own Son Jesus Christ
   Ascending into Heaven.
   Ascending into Heaven, Good Lord;
       And happy, etc.

The Coventry Carol

Coventry Mysteries

Traditional
Arr. by Sir John Stainer

Lul-lay, Thou lit-tle ti - ny Child, By, by, lul-ly, lul-lay: — Lul-
O sisters too, how may we do, For to pre-serve this day, — This
He-rod the King in his rag-ing, Charged he hath this day, — His
Then woe is me, poor Child, for Thee, And ev-er mourn and say, — For

lay, Thou lit-tle ti - ny Child, By, by, lul-ly, lul-lay. —
poor Youngling for whom we sing, By, by, lul-ly, lul-lay. —
men of might, in his own sight, All children young to slay. —
Thy part-ing nor say, nor sing, By, by, lul-ly, lul-lay. —

The Holly and the Ivy

Traditional

French
Arranged by Sir John Stainer.

1. The hol-ly and the i — vy, Now both are full well grown, Of
2. The hol-ly bears a blos-som, As white as li-ly flow'r: And
3. The hol-ly bears a ber-ry, As red as any blood; And
4. The hol-ly bears a prickle, As sharp as any thorn; And

all the trees that are in the wood, The holly bears the crown.—
Ma-ry bore sweet Je-sus Christ, To be our sweet Sav-iour.—
Ma-ry bore sweet Je-sus Christ, To do poor sinners good.—
Ma-ry bore sweet Je-sus Christ, On Christmas Day in the morn.—

Refrain

O the ris-ing of the sun, The run-ning of the deer, The playing of the merry organ, Sweet sing-ing in the quire, Sweet sing-ing in the quire.

Shepherds! Shake Off Your Sleep

Besançon Carol
Arranged by Sir John Stainer

Vivace
mf

1. Shep-herds, shake off your drowsy sleep. Rise and leave your sil-ly
2. Hark! e-ven now the bells ring round, Lis-ten to their mer-ry
3. See how the flow'rs all burst a-new Thinking snow is summer
4. Com-eth at length the age of peace, Strife and sorrow now shall
5. Shep-herds! then up and quick a-way, Seek the Babe ere break of

sheep; Angels from heav'n around loud singing, Tidings of great joy are bringing.
sound; Hark! how the birds new songs are making, As if winter's chains were breaking.
dew; See how the stars a-fresh are glowing, All their brightest beams bestowing.
cease; Prophets foretold the wondrous sto-ry Of this Heav'n-born Prince of Glo-ry.
day; He is the hope of ev-'ry na-tion, All in Him shall find salva-tion.

ff Refrain   poco rit.

Shep-herds! the chorus come and swell! Sing No-ël, O sing No-ël!

The Cherry Tree Carol

42

Traditional.

English

1. —— Jo-seph was an old man, An old man was
2. —— As they went a-walk-ing In the gar-den so
3. —— Ma-ry said to Jo-seph With her sweet lips so
4. O then —— re-plied Jo-seph With words so un-
5. —— Ma-ry said to cherry tree, "Bow down to my

he: He mar-ried sweet Ma-ry, The —— Queen of Ga-li-lee.
gay, Maid Ma-ry spied cher-ries, Hanging o-ver yon tree.
mild, "Pluck those cherries, Jo-seph, For to give to my Child."
kind, "I will pluck no cher-ries For to give to thy Child."
knee, That I may pluck cherries By —— one, two and three."

6 The uppermost sprig then
Bowed down to her knee:
"Thus you may see, Joseph,
These cherries are for me."

7. "O eat your cherries, Mary,
O eat your cherries now,
O eat your cherries, Mary,
That grow upon the bough."

8. As Joseph was a-walking
He heard Angels sing,
"This night there shall be born
Our heavenly King.

9. "He neither shall be born
In house nor in hall,
Nor in the place of Paradise,
But in an ox-stall.

The Cherry Tree Carol (Continued)

10. "He shall not be clothed
In purple nor pall;
But all in fair linen,
As wear babies all.

11. "He shall not be rocked,
In silver nor gold,
But in a wooden cradle
That rocks on the mould."

12. Mary took her Baby,
She dressed Him so sweet,
She laid Him in a manger
All there for to sleep.

13. As she stood over Him
She heard Angels sing,
"Oh! bless our dear Saviour,
Our heavenly King."

43 Christ Was Born on Christmas Day

German

1. Christ was born on Christmas Day, Wreathe the holly, twine the bay.
2. He is born to set us free, He is born our Lord to be,
3. Let the bright red berries glow, Ev'-ry where in goodly show.
4. Christian men, re-joice and sing, 'Tis the birthday of a King,

Christ-us na-tus ho-di-e; The Babe, the Son, the Ho-ly One of Ma-ry.
Ex Ma-ri-a Vir-gi-ne; The God, the Lord, by all adored for ev-er.
Christ-us na-tus ho-di-e; The Babe, the Son, the Ho-ly One of Ma-ry.
Ex Ma-ri-a Vir-gi-ne; The God, the Lord, by all adored for ev-er.

Hail To The Lord's Anointed (Continued)

3. He shall come down like showers
   Upon the fruitful earth,
   Love, joy, and hope, like flowers,
   Spring in His path to birth :
   Before Him, on the mountains,
   Shall peace, the herald go,
   And righteousness, in fountains,
   From hill to valley flow.

4. To Him shall prayer unceasing
   And daily vows ascend ;
   His kingdom still increasing,
   A kingdom without end :
   The tide of time shall never
   His covenant remove ;
   His Name shall stand for ev - er ;
   That Name to us is Love.

INDEX TO CAROLS

The Annunciation — Luke 1: 26-31